A MESSAGE FROM THE QUEENS
365 DAY ALL WOMEN AFFIRMATION COLLABORATION BOOK

2025

150 WOMEN

Copyright © 2024 R.A.G GIRL PUBLISHING
All rights reserved.
ISBN: 9798300015978

DEDICATION

To everyone that needs a word of encouragement, inspiration, and motivation to help them make it through their day.

Happiness is a choice!

Live your life, you only get one, so make it a good one!

I can only control my actions!

ACKNOWLEDGMENTS

I would like to thank and acknowledge God, for leading me to orchestrate such a beautiful, powerful and exciting assignment. Though we may have our challenges, with God, we can make it through our challenging days. God first, God last, God then, God now, God tomorrow and God forever!

I have the right to make my own choices, but I cannot control the consequences. So, I do my best to choose well.

JANAUARY

James 1:5
If any of you lack wisdom, you should pray to God, who will give it to you; because God gives generously and graciously to all.

A message from the queens

JANUARY 1

Did you know that human beings are the only species
that DO NOT follow their instincts?
We have the opportunity or misfortune to ignore our
instincts at all costs.
As we move through this year, we have the unique
opportunity to consciously listen to our
souls and bodies.
This means taking the time to slow down and tune in
to our voices,
recognizing the subtle cues that our bodies provide.
Whether it's a sense of fatigue, an
urge to create, or a feeling of joy in a particular
moment, these signals can guide us
toward a more authentic existence.

Keywanda Jackson

A message from the queens

JANUARY 2

The difference between where you are today and the miracle you seek, is you as a container of the power, glory and wisdom of the Most High God. Creation has been completed. God has made all things that you'll ever need, in your lifetime, for Godliness and a great life, abundantly available for you. You just have to be intentional in channeling your focus towards this identity. With spiritual guidance, you will live with this knowledge, this knowledge is your identity. Understand you are not alone in your life journey even if you found yourself in a remote deserted island somewhere in the middle of nowhere. Besides the trinity, you have legions of Angels, cheering you on, standing ready to assist you upon request, as you journey through this life. Goodness and mercy stand ready to follow you all the days of your life as you choose to be intentional in aligning your days with the Will and Purpose of God for your life. What is the Will of God, you may ask. It is to carry his presence with you everywhere you go, all the days of your life. How would you carry his Presence with you, you may ask. Knowing the Word of God helps you know what the presence of God is, however, carrying His presence is different for everyone. Find out what works personally for you. Do what's necessary to Find out how you can best get that Spiritual connection you need for your own benefit. Working excessive hours on a cause outside yourself is neither a virtue nor a badge of honor unless it's inner work. Besides inner work, constantly improving Sleep, Diet, Water drinking habit and physical exercise all builds you to become that Container or the version of yourself that gets your miracle.

-Dr. Bridget O. Itugbu

A message from the queens

JANUARY 3

NOTE TO SELF:
IT'S OKAY TO LOVE
ME FIRST!

-FROM THE QUEEN

A message from the queens

JANUARY 4

STOP COMPETING WITH OTHER PEOPLE! ACCEPT THE YOU THAT GOD CREATED YOU TO BE! YOU ARE PRETTY AWESOME!
TAKE THE TIME TO APPRECIATE THE AWESOME YOU!

-FROM THE QUEEN

A message from the queens

JANUARY 5

THE ENERGY YOU PUT OUT IS THE ENERGY YOU RECEIVE. SO PUT OUT GOOD ENERGY!

-FROM THE QUEEN

A message from the queens

JANUARY 6

EVERY DARK NIGHT HAS A LIGHT MORNING!
LEAN ON GOD FOR THE LIGHT IN THE NIGHT AND THANK GOD FOR THE MORNING LIGHT!

-FROM THE QUEEN

A message from the queens

JANUARY 7

Today is an amazing day to celebrate the Breath of Life. Our very existence is predicated on the very breath we breathe. This breath is a Gift from God! Thank God for the Gift of Life in this day.
Begin to celebrate your Gift of Life like never before as this is a new beginning and a wonderful time to give thanks.

-Jacquette Quashie

IG: Jacquette Qua

A message from the queens

JANUARY 8

DRIVEN....No matter the task, Achieving my goals from present to past, Every obstacle that last I quickly surpass, From Cancer to Covid I'll defeat to the end, For God chose me a devoted Angel who love him so dear, As he embrace me I fight all my fears, I challenge every obstacle in a defiant way, By keeping my family first as I humbly pray, No matter what you face, The Lord will give you Grace! AMEN!!!!

-*Maudrid Felicia Ambers*
A.K.A Doll Driven

A message from the queens

JANUARY 9

QUEEN, BE THE BEST THAT YOU CAN BE BECAUSE NO ONE IS BETTER AT BEING YOU THEN YOU

Always with love
Sista Jay Jay

Curator, Curator coach, filmmaker, life coach, acting coach, mentor, motivational speaker, author, serial entrepreneur, podcaster, actress and philanthropist, doctor
All social media: I Am Sista Jay Jay

A message from the queens

JANUARY 10

"Self-Love Affirmation"

"I am fearfully and wonderfully made by God, created in His image and loved unconditionally. I embrace my worth because Christ has redeemed me, and His love defines my value. I choose to love myself as God loves me, accepting my flaws and imperfections as part of my growth in Him. His grace covers my weaknesses, and His strength empowers me. I am precious in His sight, and I walk GODfidently, knowing that I am a child of the King. Loving myself is not an act of vanity but a necessary foundation for my sanity. I recognize that I am worthy of love, care, and respect, and this love begins within. It's not about seeking validation from the outside but nurturing the inner peace that comes from accepting who I am. The fact is through His love, I am complete, whole, and enough just as am...and so are you.

-*Carla Langford*

A message from the queens

JANUARY 11

THERE IS NO COMPETITION FOR WHAT IS FOR YOU. NEVER COMPETE WITH SOMEONE THAT WANTS WHAT IS YOURS. STAY FOCUS AND WALK IN THE KNOWINGNESS THAT NO ONE CAN TAKE WHAT GOD HAS GIVEN YOU. AND IF THEY TAKE IT, THEN IT WAS NOT YOURS.
THANK GOD FOR THE FREEDOM TO RECEIVE WHAT IS FOR YOU AND LET GO OF WHAT IS NOT FOR YOU.

-FROM THE QUEEN

A message from the queens

JANUARY 12

Yes, You!
Scripture: Judges 6:14-16 NKV
14 Then the Lord turned to him and said, "Go in this might of yours, and you shall save Israel from the hand of the Midianites. Have I not sent you?" **15** So he said to Him, "O [d]my Lord, how can I save Israel? Indeed my clan *is* the weakest in Manasseh, and I *am* the least in my father's house." **16** And the Lord said to him, "Surely I will be with you, and you shall defeat the Midianites as one man."

Have you ever felt like Gideon did in this scripture? God had already declared him a mighty man of valor although he was hiding in fear of the Midianites and threshing wheat in the winepress. When God called him to save Israel, Gideon's response was a laundry list of reasons of excuses. Does this sound familiar? God has called you to a mission or task and your initial r
esponse might be doubting your own worth and why you aren't qualified. Maybe you're a former drug addict, were a teenage mother, someone who grew up without a father, divorced or didn't grow up in church. But, Elohim, God the creator who knew you before you were formed in your mother's womb is aware of all your struggles. He knows your past, your insecurities, and your flaws. Yet, He still chose you, wants to use you to spread the gospel, and inspire others. God knows your abilities and has gifted you uniquely. He sees your potential, has ordained and sanctified you for this purpose. Most importantly, just as he assured Gideon, He is with you. You don't have to be perfect; you just need to be willing, available, and obedient. So today, I encourage you to let go of all your excuses and fears. Say yes to God's call. Trust in Him and let Him use you for His glory.
-*Evg. Jacci Thomas*

A message from the queens

JANUARY 13

FAITH IT until you MAKE IT!

With love from Della A FaithfulSpirit Brooks

JANUARY 14

SOMETIMES THE BATTLE IS IN YOUR MIND.
USE THE WEAPON OF PEACE TO WIN THE FIGHT.

-FROM THE QUEEN

A message from the queens

JANUARY 15

SOMETIMES THE LOUDEST VOICE IS A CLOSED MOUTH!

-FROM THE QUEEN

A message from the queens

JANUARY 16

Note To Self

You are worthy
You are kind
You are beautiful
You are smart

You are your Creators canvas
His work of art

You are loved
You are talented
Your being is no mistake

There is purpose for your life
Self-doubt has no place

Peace & Blessings,

-Charnora Reid
children's author

www.charnorareid.com
charnorareid@gmail.com

A message from the queens

JANUARY 17

God is my guide and protector
I desire peace and love into my life
I am more than enough
I believe in myself and my abilities
I respect and love myself for who I am
I overcome all of life's obstacles
I forgive myself for my mistakes
I am a better me every day

Speak these affirmations into your mind and spirit….as a man or woman thinketh so is she.

-KaRhonda Hines

IG: kaykay_borngreat
Website:www.karhondahines.com

A message from the queens

JANUARY 18

SOMETIMES YOU MUST BE WILLING TO LOSE, IN ORDER TO WIN!

-FROM THE QUEEN

A message from the queens

JANUARY 19

Gratitude is my lifestyle.

-*Jakinda Gibbs*
A.K.A
Doll Gratitude

A message from the queens

JANUARY 20

COMMUNICATION IS THE ANTIDOTE TO MISUNDERSTANDING!

-FROM THE QUEEN

JANUARY 21

FORGIVENESS DOESN'T MAKE THE WRONG RIGHT, IT RELEASES YOU FROM THE BURDEN OF THE OFFENSE.

-FROM THE QUEEN

A message from the queens

JANUARY 22

I AM
Woman
Black
Blessed
Beautiful
Brave
Beneficent
Brilliant
Bubbly

-Paula Williams A.K.A Doll Zinnia

A message from the queens

JANUARY 23

ACCOUNTABILITY IS A SIGN OF MATURITY AND THE PRECRIPTION TO PROCRASTINATION.

-FROM THE QUEEN

A message from the queens

JANUARY 24

KIND WORDS ARE LIKE HONEY TO TEA WHILE HARSH WORDS ARE LIKE A BRICK FALLING ON YOUR TOE.

-FROM THE QUEEN

A message from the queens

JANUARY 25

A BROKEN PROMISE IS MORE HARMFUL THAN THE HURTFUL TRUTH.

-FROM THE QUEEN

A message from the queens

JANUARY 26

IT IS BETTER TO LIVE DEBT FREE WITHIN YOUR MEANS THAN TO GO BROKE TRYING TO LIVE IN A FANTASY.

-FROM THE QUEEN

JANUARY 27

I am a powerful, radiant force, embodying divine light. The universe flows through me, fueling my limitless strength, courage, and grace. I am destined to manifest my dreams. Fearless, aligned with my highest purpose, I trust the divine plan. I am healthy, abundant, wise, and eternally blessed.

From the desk of *Diamond Tee*

IG/TicTok: Tangirce
FB/Twitter: Tandylyn Cooke

JANUARY 28

THE ONLY PERSON THAT CAN STOP YOU IS YOU. NO ONE HAS THE POWER TO STOP YOU. THAT POWER BELONGS TO YOU. PEOPLE CAN THROW OBSTACLES YOUR WAY BUT YOU HAVE THE POWER TO OVERCOME THEM ALL!

-FROM THE QUEEN

A message from the queens

JANUARY 29

DEAL WITH PEOPLE ON THE LEVEL THAT THEY ARE ON AND NOT THE LEVEL YOU WANT THEM ON.

-FROM THE QUEEN

A message from the queens

JANUARY 30

THE BIGGEST MISTAKE YOU CAN MAKE ON YOUR JOURNEY TO SUCCESS IS WAITING FOR SOMEONE TO BELIEVE IN YOU.

-FROM THE QUEEN

JANUARY 31

Love the people that want your love and love them with all of your might.

-From the Queen

FEBRUARY

Isaiah 40:31
But those who hope in the Lord will renew their strength. They will soar on wings like eagles; they will run and not grow weary; they will walk and not be faint.

A message from the queens

FEBRUARY 1

BE GOOD
DO GOOD
FEEL GOOD
LOOK GOOD
NO MATTER WHAT IT
LOOKS LIKE
SEE GOOD

-FROM THE QUEEN

FEBRUARY 2

When life begin to life and try to take a tow on me, I simply remember that:
I can do all things through Christ who strengthens me.
I hope this encourages you to keep going!

-*Adrianne Greene*

A message from the queens

FEBRUARY 3

Remember
God is with you always….
Loving and Forgiving
Guiding and Directing
Caring and Protecting
And Blessings Everything
You Do!

-Loretta Hickson

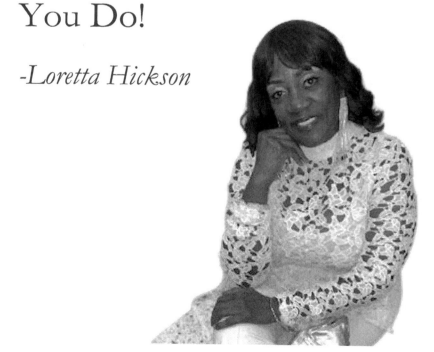

A message from the queens

FEBRUARY 4

The love I have for myself increases my capacity to love others.

-Tracey Davis
A.K.A
Doll Precious

A message from the queens

FEBRUARY 5

I am in charge of my life story. No one controls my destiny. I am in charge of my life story.

-Baloay Stokes

A message from the queens

FEBRUARY 6

Hey sis! You're loved and capable of overcoming it all.

-*KIESHLA RUFFIN*

FEBRUARY 7

A person's action will always speak the truth of the heart.

Believe the heartbeat.

-From the Queen

FEBRUARY 8

A kind word can save someone's life. Be kind with your words and let your words bring a smile on a sad soul.

-From the Queen

A message from the queens

FEBRUARY 9

Be the person that others love to see come and hate to see go.

-From the Queen

FEBRUARY 10

I'm responsible for my own happiness!

SO

I think outside the box that I'm living in! What may seem unorthodox may be the answer to my dilemma.

-Jakinda Gibb
A.K.A
Doll Gratitude
And
The Queen

A message from the queens

FEBRUARY 11

Do not let your words be like the waves of the sea. But rather let your character be rooted like an oak tree.

-From the Queen

A message from the queens

FEBRUARY 12

You are amazing!! Yes, you! Just a quick reminder that you can do whatever you put your mind to. Don't be afraid to step outside the box and try something new. You will never know where it will take. Do not worry about the would've, could've and should've. Just do it, do it and be proud that you did it!

-Lizette M Diaz
Facebook: Liz Diaz
Instagram: leedreamzz

A message from the queens

FEBRUARY 13

Love is like a puzzle. You don't have to force it. If it's the right piece, it will fit on its own.

-From the Queen

A message from the queens

FEBRUARY 14

A STAGNANT LIFE STUNTS YOUR GROWTH; FREE YOUR MIND TO ACTION AND OUTGROW YOURSELF.

The end…of a new beginning!

-Felicia "Transition" Winston

A message from the queens

FEBRUARY 15

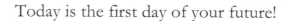

Let me encourage you,

Today is the first day of your future!

No matter how hard we try we will never be able to change anything that has already happened BUT we do have the present moment to make better choices and decisions for the future. So don't allow the smoke from your past to cloud your vision of your future. Think and see clearly. Don't let what happened or didn't happen to take control of what is or what is to come. You've been waiting on God to move but God's been waiting on you to move. You were created for and are still here for a purpose. Keep the mission mind no matter what rises against you, God is still in control. Don't let your opposition move you from your position. No matter what battle you're facing stand on the word of God.

Reminder for the day:

God loves you. There's nothing you've done, doing, or will do that can change that. You're imperfect, He knows. You're broken, He knows. You're hurting, He knows. You're angry, He knows. You're a sinner, He knows.

HE STILL LOVES YOU AND WANTS TO HEAL YOU, IF YOU LET HIM!

LouCinda B
FB: LouCinda No Regrets
IG: @i_bloom2

A message from the queens

FEBRUARY 16

I am strong, capable, and worthy of all the success and happiness I seek. My voice matters, and I embrace my unique journey with confidence.

-Mia Williams
FB: Miaw
IG: @justmiathemodel

A message from the queens

FEBRUARY 17

My Sisters,

Dr. Kimberly Simmons Dean

As you navigate the journey of life, remember that you are divinely crafted with a unique purpose. Your spirit is a wellspring of resilience and grace, capable of overcoming any challenge that comes your way. In moments of doubt, let faith be your anchor. Trust that you are guided by a higher power that knows the path even when you do not. Embrace the beauty of your journey, understanding that every step, whether triumphant or difficult, is shaping you into the remarkable woman you are meant to be. Surround yourself with positivity and love. Seek out the voices that uplift you and align with the values you hold. Know that you are never alone on this path; a community of supportive sisters and spiritual guides walks beside you. Take time to nurture your soul.

Whether through prayer, meditation, or quiet reflection, connect with the divine energy within you. Let it fill you with strength, wisdom, and the courage to pursue your dreams. You are powerful beyond measure, and the world needs the light only you can bring. Trust in your abilities, embrace your worth, and know that you are destined for greatness. Continue to shine brightly and inspire others with your unwavering spirit. As we all know no one is perfect but continue my sisters to strive to be as close as possible. Allow your confidence to remain high and your standards to match. Walk in Faith and allow God to guide your steps. You will not always understand the burdens that you will have to carry but continue to push through this test of life. Woman of greatness who is reading this message when you are feeling low, read this message again, and believe in yourself as well as the inner strength that God put in you to always walk in greatness.

You are beautiful and wonderfully made.

A message from the queens

FEBRUARY 18

No one should love you more than you love yourself.

-From the Queen

A message from the queens

FEBRUARY 19

Success starts in the mind. Condition your mind to succeed and let nothing change your mind.

-From the Queen

A message from the queens

FEBRUARY 20

I will love myself in a judgement free zone. I know my worth and value plus tax. I prioritize my Mind, body and spirit. I can unapologetically put myself first. I ooze with appeal. I am happy and full. I have more than I need. I articulate my needs, wants and desires. I speak up and speak out for myself. Life has made me brave; I have overcome my fears by stepping out of my comfort zone. My self-control gets stronger every day. I forgive myself. I give myself grace. I don't make mistakes I learn lessons. I will keep an open heart. I will not compare my journey with anyone else's. I am a special blend and sculpted to perfection. I am grateful and thankful. My wounds have made me intentional. My scars have brightened my light. I am a testimony of God's love and favor.

-*Tammy Michelle*

A message from the queens

FEBRUARY 21

Take the time to smile today
Take the time to be happy today
Take the time to tell someone that you love them today
Take the time to love yourself today
Take the time to take care of you today
Take the time to relax today
Take the time to think today
Take the time to see things from a different lens today
Take the time to learn something new today
Take the time to forgive today
Take the time to be a better you today

-From the Queen

FEBRUARY 22

Mind the business that pays you and not the business that pays others. You'll find your life less stressful.

-From the Queen

A message from the queens

FEBRUARY 23

You are a force to be reckoned with, a queen who reigns with love, dignity, and power.

-*Latricia Muhammad*
A.K.A
Doll Exquisite

A message from the queens

FEBRUARY 24

Real love never every hurts.
Remember that.

-From the Queen

A message from the queens

FEBRUARY 25

Love is NOT manipulative
Love is NOT controlling
Love is NOT violent
Love is NOT hurtful
Love is NOT mean
Love is NOT a liar
Love is NOT a cheater
Love is NOT angry
Love is NOT ugly
Love is NOT untrusting

Now that you know what love is not, do not allow yourself to be treated as such.

YOU DESERVE TO BE LOVED IN A HEALTHY MANNER.

-From the Queen

A message from the queens

FEBRUARY 26

Nothing can dim the light that shines from within.

Blu' Bolton

A message from the queens

FEBRUARY 27

Treat people the way you want to be treated. Kindness is contagious.

It is so easy to fall into the trap of responding negatively to people, especially when they are being rude or ugly to you.

Try returning their negativity or rudeness with kindness. Maybe they will follow your example.

-From the desk of *Rita Parker*

Facebook: Rita Moyer Parker
IG: @rpconfidential

A message from the queens

FEBRUARY 28

The only person that you can control is yourself. Practice it until you perfect it.

-From the Queen

MARCH

Lamentations 3:22-24
Because of the Lord's great love we are not consumed, for his compassions never fail. They are new every morning; great is your faithfulness.

A message from the queens

MARCH 1

Enjoy life more
Stress less even more
Trust God even the more

-From the Queen

A message from the queens

MARCH 2

To all young relationships out there, love one another. Argue less and talk more. Say "I love You" every day. Enjoy life together, you never know what moment may be your last.

With love: Hershai James

A message from the queens

MARCH 3

Do not be a know it all because a know it all give no room to learn it all.

-From the Queen

A message from the queens

MARCH 4

It's good to be alive but it's even better to live.

-Kieshia Ruffin

A message from the queens

MARCH 5

Your uniqueness is what makes you special!

-Marnie Edge
A.K.A
Doll Sunlight

A message from the queens

MARCH 6

Patience is golden, and God's timing is perfect! Remember this as you embrace the challenges of life.

-*Della* AfaithfulSpirit *Brooks*

MARCH 7

Every 'no' is not to harm you.
AND
Every 'yes' is not to help you.
Let God reveal to you the reason behind each.

-From the Queen

A message from the queens

MARCH 8

Queen, remember that your strength is unmatched, your grace is undeniable, and your potential is limitless.

-*Wendy Conley* A.K.A Doll Fabulouz

A message from the queens

MARCH 9

Knowledge is only power when it is used. Otherwise, it's just powerless information.

-From the Queen

A message from the queens

MARCH 10

When life serves you a sour apple. Throw it away and get some good apples.

-From the Queen

MARCH 11

Most people say they always talk to God but how many actually listen to Him?

-From the Queen

A message from the queens

MARCH 12

It takes a strong person to ask for forgiveness, but it takes a stronger person to actually forgive.

-From the Queen

A message from the queens

MARCH 13

I... am Her, who have been in the poorest of states, far from the pearly gates at a time when the world was filled with so much hate. I know few can relate.

Pushing aside all of the stereotypes between black and white, to the choices I made, whether wrong or right.

I ... am Her, who've crawled from the depths of the abyss, broken from unmartial bliss. Yet focused on the lantern lit in the thickness of the mist.

Taking aim, while taking shots from physical torment and mental abuse to a place I had seemly forgotten about.

I... am Her, mother of three children. Two boys and one girl showing that there was more to live for in this vast cruel world.

Taking an oath to protect against all enemies, foreign and domestic when domestic became daily from the hands of the man I married and was so in love with.

I...am Her, who excelled in school, retired from the Army, yet still covered in shame, hiding from hurt, running from truths, trying to escape the realms of pain.

A woman of color, built by structure, my pride I won't hide as Maya Angelou wrote and spoke" Still I Rise"

I...am Her, saying to you" Look at Me Now". To all women who forgotten how to be true to yourself, be bold, beautiful and strong, to keep going forward when you feel it's too much to carry on.

Be who you dare to be, asking Jesus to take the wheel believing he died for you upon Calvary Hill.

I...am Her, who let go and eventually let God. Diagnosed with breast cancer to an unknown brain aneurysm. Look at Me Now!

From the beat of my heart, the core of my soul, and the very air that I breathe, telling you o' spread your wings and fly free. Don't give in nor give up. Just become HER, who chose to believe... For I am Her, A QUEEN!

-Lisa James

A message from the queens

MARCH 14

I am the embodiment of resilience, grace, and power. My history is woven with strength, my presence demands respect, and my future is limitless. I honor the beauty of my skin, the wisdom of my ancestors, and the courage in my heart. Every challenge I face, I overcome with dignity, for I am a queen, rooted in legacy, flourishing in purpose, and unstoppable in my journey. My voice, my dreams, and my strength matter, and I rise, every day, knowing I am enough!

Sandi Pruitt
SEPruitt Consulting
Facebook: Sandi Pruitt

A message from the queens

MARCH 15

Women should lift each other up and be an encouragement to another.
But don't wait for those moments to come, take the chance and make them happen.
Be fearless and be strong and encourage yourself.

Ashley Clark

A message from the queens

MARCH 16

Some things cannot be taken back or reversed once it's done. Words being one.

-From the Queen

A message from the queens

MARCH 17

Never make emotional decisions.

-From the Queen

A message from the queens

MARCH 18

Greatness comes from within, stand strong in yourself. Trust your inner being the greatness is within you.

Katrina Monroe-Pettway
A.K.A
Doll Diligent

A message from the queens

MARCH 19

The truth is always better than the lie. Be bold enough to accept the truth and reject the lie.

-From the Queen

A message from the queens

MARCH 20

Never count yourself out. Sometimes you have to be your own cheerleader.

-From the Queen

A message from the queens

MARCH 21

Look at You
 Strong (*Black*) Women
  YOU made it
   through it ALL.

Now walk PROUDLY with your HEAD UP!

-Shannel Lundy

A message from the queens

MARCH 22

Never let your peace be infiltrated.

-From the Queen

A message from the queens

MARCH 23

A car only moves when you start the engine and press the gas. It stops when you hit the brakes.

The Moral to this statement is:

No one can stop your destiny, but you, so keep pressing the gas.

-From the Queen

A message from the queens

MARCH 24

Complaints and happiness do not share the same space.

-From the Queen

A message from the queens

MARCH 25

Life is what you make it.
So, make it a good one starting with today.

-From the Queen

A message from the queens

MARCH 26

Holding on to the past keeps you from embracing the present and grasping the future.

-From the Queen

A message from the queens

MARCH 27

It is wise to focused on getting it right rather than being right.

-From the Queen

A message from the queens

MARCH 28

There is more to life than money.
Your time is something you cannot get back, replace, or play make up.
So, take some time for you, yourself and I.
If you don't value self no one else will.
Be okay with loving you first.

-Akilah Dixon

MARCH 29

I am comfortable being me.
No, I am not perfect,
but I am perfect for me.

-From the Queen

MARCH 30

Cooler heads always prevail over heated words.

-From the Queen

A message from the queens

MARCH 31

Remember this:
Family, Faith and Finances which equals Freedom.

LaToya Young
Instagram- latoyaayoung
Upscale wine & more –
Facebook
Upscalewineandmore.com

APRIL

Romans 15:13
May the God of hope fill you with all joy and peace as you trust in Him, so that you may overflow with hope by the power of the Holy Spirit.

APRIL 1

LOVING YOU IS THE BEST GIFT THAT YOU CAN GIVE YOURSELF.

-From the Queen

A message from the queens

APRIL 2

Find Your Peace

As women we are usually making sure everyone around us is okay. We have to make time for ourselves. I like going to the beach because it gives me peace. I like to listen to the waves. Find your peace and hold on to it.

-RITA PARKER

A message from the queens

APRIL 3

Listening
is
fundamental.

-FROM THE QUEEN

A message from the queens

APRIL 4

Too bless to be stressed sometimes you just have to encourage yourself.

-Suzann White
A.K.A
Doll Happiness

APRIL 5

Which are you more concern with? The message or the messenger.

-From the Queen

APRIL 6

Less time spent on other people affairs is more growth for your own.

-From the Queen

APRIL 7

Accepting that you cannot control others releases so much stress in your life.

-From the Queen

APRIL 8

Some trails are to test your strength, others are a sign that you should change your course.
Seek God to know the difference.

-From the Queen

A message from the queens

APRIL 9

Celebrate yourself today, you deserve it.

-Telisha M. Harris

A message from the queens

APRIL 10

We are all on this journey called life. You never know what direction it will take you, but always be kind no matter the direction.

-Tracie Frank

APRIL 11

Every day may not be your best day, but you have the power to make every day a good day.

-From the Queen

A message from the queens

APRIL 12

Misery loves company, but I keep ignoring the invite.

-Robin Curry

A message from the queens

APRIL 13

Do not waste your time trying to prove yourself to someone who will never approve you.

-From the Queen

APRIL 14

The person who rejects correction is the person who will never grow.

-From the Queen

A message from the queens

APRIL 15

Keeping your peace in the mist of chaos shows God you are listening.

-From the Queen

A message from the queens

APRIL 16

Every thought should not always be spoken.

-From the Queen

A message from the queens

APRIL 17

Just because you can does not mean that you should.

-From the Queen

A message from the queens

APRIL 18

People are going to be people; I can't make them change. I can only change me. And I cannot allow people to make me upset.

-Storme Burns

A message from the queens

APRIL 19

It's okay to say I need help.

-From the Queen

A message from the queens

APRIL 20

I was shattered, a fragment of my former self, but somehow, in the midst of my brokenness, God gave me the strength to rediscover who I truly was. In those moments when hope seemed distant and elusive, I turned my eyes to the Lord, the source of my help and the wellspring of my strength.

Life, to me, is like a personal movie, and I am the writer of its script. There was a time when I was utterly lost, wandering aimlessly through the scenes of my life. But in that darkness, I heard a gentle whisper—a voice that spoke directly to my heart. It told me, "I don't like that scene in your movie. Erase it and rewrite it."

That moment marked the beginning of a profound transformation. I learned how to love myself, truly and deeply. I realized that if I could continue to live in this world after losing someone I loved dearly, then I was far stronger than I had ever imagined.

So, when you find yourself lost or heartbroken, remember this: God never allows more hurt or pain than we can bear. And always remember, this is your movie, your script. You have the power to change the scenes you don't like. You are the author of your own story, and with God's guidance, you can rewrite it into something beautiful.

Peace & Blessings,
Tameca Ricks

A message from the queens

APRIL 21

Be happy
Be sad
Be joyful
Be angry
Be nice
Be mean
Be forgiving
Be vengeful
Be loved
Be hated
YOU CHOOSE
what you will
BE!

-From the Queen

A message from the queens

APRIL 22

I am a beautiful, determined and powerful *(black)* woman. I have overcome many obstacles and my light shines brightly.
I am Still Standing.

Thank you, Lord.
Audrey Harris
A.K.A
Still Standing

APRIL 23

Do not measure wisdom with a person's charisma, fashion or style. Wisdom has no preference.

-From the Queen

A message from the queens

APRIL 24

True confidence does not down others.

-*From the Queen*

APRIL 25

Thoughts and emotions rarely travel at the same speed. I've learned it is wise to slow down and let them catch up with each other before speaking.

**Monica Guillory,
Founder Back Pocket Wisdom, LLC**

www.backpocketwisdom.net

A message from the queens

APRIL 26

The longer I live the more I realize that life is a journey. A journey has twists and turns, ups and downs, wins and losses, joy and pain, love and hatred. No matter what part of the journey you are in, the most important thing is to keep living, because life will never stop lifing so you should never stop living life. God's plan for us is set and if we follow HIS plan, no matter what life throws our way,
    ALL THINGS WILL WORK TOGETHER FOR OUR GOOD! BLESSINGS!

-Cassandra Greene
Philanthropist
Ordained Minister
W.O.W.W Ministry
Director
Actor
Author

A message from the queens

APRIL 27

I am turning my dreams into reality
I am turning can'ts into can's
I am turning my fears into courage
I am turning my shyness into boldness
I am turning my weakness into strengths.
I am turning my chaos into peace
I am turning my negativities into positivity's
I am turning my lack into bountiful
I am turning my need to have
I am turning my venges to forgiveness
I am turning my hate in love
I am turning my failures into wins
I am turning my heartbreaks into healing
I am turning my confusion into understanding
I am turning my quick temper into calm results
I am turning my procrastination to progression

-From the Queen

APRIL 28

A wounded wolf will welcome your help, yet he will attack you as soon as he is able to.
Be mindful of the people with wolf spirits that you are led to help.

-From the Queen

A message from the queens

APRIL 29

My strength, wisdom, and grace inspire others to rise with me.

−From Tonya Edwards A.K.A Doll TeTe

A message from the queens

APRIL 30

When a person's season is up, be at peace with it.

-From the Queen

MAY

Romans 15:13
"May the God of hope fill you with all joy and peace as you trust in him, so that you may overflow with hope by the power of the Holy Spirit".

A message from the queens

MAY 1

BUYAH!
It's Done!
BUYAH!
Be Unique!
BUYAH!
Repeat this every day to yourself
I AM A DIAMOND!
BUYAH!
Now say BUYAH out loud! Doesn't is make you want to smile?
If not, say it again!
BUYAH!
Remember you and I are DIAMONDS!
BUYAH!

-Carolyn Wesley Stith

A message from the queens

MAY 2

Take the time to count your blessings. They are usually more than your complaints.

-From the Queen

MAY 3

In the mist of my sorrow, trouble, uneasiness, pain, hurt, grief, fear, distress and discomfort, I will remember:

2 Thessalonians 3:16
"Now may the Lord of peace himself give you peace at all times and in every way. The Lord be with all of you".

-From the Queen

MAY 4

I will celebrate God as if He already did it.
I will be thankful however He does it.
I will praise Him even if it's not how I imagine it to be.

-From the Queen

A message from the queens

MAY 5

BELIEVE IN YOURSELF
SAY THIS WITH ME.

I believe in myself because if I don't believe in myself no one else will. I have confidence that I will become as wealthy as I set my goals to be. I will always stay positive with my thoughts and decisions on my path through life.

I AM UNSTOPPABLE

I will be focused on the things that matter to me. My life will be surrounded with greatness, wealth, love, and great relationships. I will be strong and determined so that my hard work will pay off. My faith will keep me going for a lifetime as long as I continue to make the right choices for me.

I GOT THIS!

Facebook: Randle Tisha
MrsteeMcc Master McCullough

IG: Tee2unikk

A message from the queens

MAY 6

I will activate my faith by trusting God while I'm doing the work towards the manifestation.

-From the Queen

A message from the queens

MAY 7

Faith has no fear. Fear has no faith. But the fearful that walks in faith overcomes fear through their faithfulness.

*−From the Queen
and
Della AfaithfulSpirit Brooks*

MAY 8

Being the loudest person in the room does not mean you are the smartest. It just makes you the loudest.

-From the Queen

A message from the queens

MAY 9

Sometimes your help may come in the most unexpected form. Be ready to receive it.

-From the Queen

MAY 10

-Everything happens for a reason.
-The will of GOD will never take me where grace of GOD will not protect me.
-God refuses to leave me the way he found me.
-P.U.S.H (Pray Until Something Happens)
-GOD will develop me in his purpose.

Trust God, I do!
-*NaiCora Lewis*

A message from the queens

MAY 11

Love is a rinse and repeat cycle. As your give it, you should be receiving it.

-From the Queen

A message from the queens

MAY 12

Get to know yourself, celebrate your existence and be happy with who are.

-From the Queen

A message from the queens

MAY 13

I live off a mustard seed of faith

When I'm running my miles as I do 4 days a week. I put my gospel music in my ear, and I go into meditation. I say to myself, Self, you have total control over this day and all of your thoughts. The things that mean you no good, toss them away. I'm going to be wonderful to myself and no one will harm me with their words or actions.
Self you are a woman that has endured quite of bit of pain. However, you have turned that pain into happiness. Don't allow it to consume you. You have work to do.
Me and your inner self adore you.

-*Tonya Lewis*

A message from the queens

MAY 14

Your imperfections makes you unique. Embrace you!

-From the Queen

A message from the queens

MAY 15

Hey sis,

Let me tell you something important— comparison is a straight-up thief. It'll steal your happiness if you let it. Stop worrying about what everyone else is doing or how far ahead they seem. You've got your own path, and it's yours for a reason. Time? It's not waiting for anyone, so why wait to chase your dreams? Yeah, love and relationships can come when the time is right, but what about your goals? They need you now. Procrastinating only sets you back, and you don't want to look back one day wishing you'd started sooner. Here's the thing: if you spend your life watching someone else's journey, you'll completely miss the beauty of your own. Your life is happening right now, and it's full of opportunities that are meant just for you. Don't sleep on that! At the end of the day, the only person who was with you when you came into this world, and who'll be with you when you leave, is you. So, sis, put yourself first, trust your gut, and take those steps. The 'perfect moment' isn't coming—you have to create it. You got this.

SHE ISN'T WAITING ON PERFECT. SHE'S CREATING IT.

MIKAYLA JOHNSON

A message from the queens

MAY 16

Never apologize for being blessed.

-From the Queen

A message from the queens

MAY 17

HELLO? CAN YOU HEAR ME? YOU GOT THIS!

Keep God First! Never allow your past to define your future! You were born a conqueror! You have a purpose! Don't operate in fear! Stay focused! Self-motivation is vital to success! Be patient with yourself!

AND WHATEVER YOU DO, DON'T GIVE UP!

Love,
Monaneka
"Mona J" Jones-Moore

IG:
@Mona.J.TheCenterOfAttention

www.Mona-J.com

A message from the queens

MAY 18

You are beautiful. Remember that!

-From the Queen

A message from the queens

MAY 19

I WILL be the reason a person smile THIS DAY!

From the desk of
Sophia Johnson

Facebook:
Sophia Johnson
IG: SophiaJ1965

A message from the queens

MAY 20

I give myself grace, mutual respect and genuine compassion.

-Tawana Robinson
A.K.A
Doll Versatile

A message from the queens

MAY 21

Expressing gratitude can have mental and physical benefits such as:

1. Reducing anxiety
2. Helping with depression
3. Changing negative thinking
4. Cultivating a positive self-image

- Traci Frank

A message from the queens

MAY 22

Do your best,
Be the best,
You are the best.
Now SHINE, SHINE, SHINE!

-Marlinda Lewis
A.K.A
Doll Gorgeous

A message from the queens

MAY 23

Repeat this until you believe it:

I like me.

-From the Queen

A message from the queens

MAY 24

Today I will not let anyone else tell me who I am. I have no control over what someone says does or thinks about me. ONLY how I respond!

-*Tiwana R. Jefferies*
A.K.A
Doll Lady Grey

A message from the queens

MAY 25

Let your love shine in the hearts of all whom you come in contact with.

-From the Queen

A message from the queens

MAY 26

Being me is how I win. I am becoming a better version of myself each day and the love I have for myself increases my capacity to love others.

Love,
Towanna Crawford
A.K.A
Doll GiGi

A message from the queens

MAY 27

Dear Sister, you are his focus. Allow yourself to feel *HIS LOVE* today.

-*Kwana King Stark*

MAY 28

I'm a child of God, an original, exactly who he created me to be. I am fearfully and wonderfully made. My weaknesses and failures are greater opportunities for growth, beautiful pathways for God's light to shine. God loves me and I am more than enough. I'm his masterpiece.

-Constance Moseley

A message from the queens

MAY 29

Let the memories of you be pleasant in other people's memory.

-From the Queen

A message from the queens

MAY 30

I'm lifted
I'm gifted
I have no limits.
I focus on the future, where there is hope and not the past of sorrow and regret.

-Vontessia Nosike
IG: nikkynine9

A message from the queens

MAY 31

If someone sends a negative report about you, let your actions, and your character be your response.

-From the Queen

# JUNE

Numbers 6:24-26

May the LORD bless you and protect you. May the LORD smile on you and be gracious to you. May the LORD show you his favor and give you, his peace.

A message from the queens

JUNE 1

Learning to trust God is a taught behavior. We're students in His class. Keep the Faith.

- Algena Lomax

A message from the queens

JUNE 2

To love is one thing
To be loved is another
But to be loved and to
love is the
very best thing!

-From the Queen

A message from the queens

JUNE 3

In all of the world there is none like you. Let your presence be remembered in a way that all who come in contact with you be blessed.

-From the Queen

A message from the queens

JUNE 4

It hurts when you want what you deserve heart. Lift your heart and soul to God and He will help you create what you don't have. Trust him.

Akella

A message from the queens

JUNE 5

Beautiful Bold Woman

You were carried in your mother's womb for many months. You made your debut some time ago. A beautiful, fearless woman you are. Your mother gave birth to a little princess, but you grew into the queen you are today.

You are the picture of beauty

God designed you perfectly. Born unbroken, crawling until one day you were able to walk. Standing tall. staring at yourself in the mirror. What do you see? Right, a God fearing, challenge winning. beautiful woman.

Never

Let any challenge break you beautiful woman. Obstacles may be your story but overcoming them will be your testimony. Giving up is not an option, finding your purpose will be the only answer.

You will win Sister

You will graduate you next test. You will exceed your own expectations. You will graduate college, something that has never been achieved in your family. You will accomplish what you set out to do. Just speak it, allow nothing contrary to your vision to come out of your mouth.

Bold and Furious

Never let the hurt from a man, rape you from the promise God has for you. Exemplify your greatness. I'm referring to the queen inside of you. You're more than what your mother and father said you would be. Or the spoken words your pimp claiming that you will always be his number one curbside prostitute. You're better than falling to the devilish streets as another addict lost in this world. Wake up, fight your way through the demonic ties of your family bloodline. Be you, a beautiful, bold, liberated, woman.

Proverbs 14:1
Every wise woman buildeth her house: but the foolish plucketh it down with her hands.
Proverbs 3:5-6
Trust in the LORD with all thine heart; and lean not unto thine own understanding. In all thy ways acknowledge him, and he shall direct thy paths.   *-Angel Dandridge-Riddick*

A message from the queens

JUNE 6

I am
Loving
Love
Lovable

-Beverly Brown

A message from the queens

JUNE 7

I am easy to talk to,
I am easy to be liked,
I am easy to love,
I am easy to be loved.

-From the Queen

JUNE 8

There are choices we must make in life. Some are easier to make but the harder ones are usually because we can not control the outcome. Trust your heart that what you have no control of God will give you strength to choose wisely.

-From the Queen

A message from the queens

JUNE 9

We live for today, because yesterday is gone. Positive Energy!

-*Marguerite Wilkes*

A message from the queens

JUNE 10

A LETTER TO MY SISTER FRIEND

Dear Sister Friend,

I hope this letter finds you surrounded by love and warmth. I wanted to take a moment to remind you of the incredible person you are and how much you mean to me.

Your radiant spirit and unwavering strength have been evident. Your kindness touches everyone around you, and your resilience in the face of challenges is truly inspiring. Every conversation you share, every laugh, every tear—each moment reaffirms just what a truly amazing woman you are!!

Remember, it's okay to have days when you feel less than your best. But always know that within you lies a reservoir of strength, courage, and beauty that shines through, even on the cloudiest days. Your dreams are valid, your feelings are important, and your presence in this world makes it a better place.

Never doubt your worth or the positive impact you have on those around you. I believe in you wholeheartedly, and I'm here to support you every step of the way.

Thank you for being the incredible sister-friend that you are.

With all my love and admiration,
Tammy D. Taylor

www.tammydtaylor.com
FB: Tammy D Taylor
IG: Tammydtaylor_thebrand

A message from the queens

JUNE 11

In life you may fall. When you do fall don't be so quick to jump up. Take a moment and understand why you fell and take the necessary steps to not repeat the same fall when you get up.

-From the Queen

JUNE 12

Keep shining. Someone is depending on your light!

-From the Queen

A message from the queens

JUNE 13

Be the person that made the decision to go for it!

-From the Queen

A message from the queens

JUNE 14

You have to believe in yourself when no one else does. Never be limited by other people's limited imaginations!

Yours Truly
Sencere

FB: La Nitra White-Rucker

A message from the queens

JUNE 15

I SHALL...

I shall walk in who God called me to be.
I shall build a legacy for my children and
Children's children.
I shall be healed from all past trauma and
delivered of life lessons.

-Pauline 'Doll Chosen' Alves

JUNE 16

I will not all my past to dictate my present or my future.
I will surround myself around positive people doing positive things.
I will not allow anyone to tell me that I am not worthy.
I will not listen to gossip about someone else because I understand that if they gossip about others to me, they will gossip about me to them.
I will fill my mind with positivity, good energy, and love.
I will succeed in everything, I set my mind to do that God has ordain for me to do.
I will talk to, lean on and talk to God every day and every in step of my journey.
I will live a long life in good health, prosperity, faith, joyful, love, and in both spiritual and physical wealth.

-Sista Jay Jay

A message from the queens

JUNE 17

One of the best outfits you can put on today is: CONFIDENCE! Wear it well!

-From the Queen

JUNE 18

Do today what will make you proud tomorrow!

-From the Queen

A message from the queens

JUNE 19

Do not listen to anyone telling you what you cannot do!

-From the Queen

JUNE 20

Be the type of person you would admire!

-From the Queen

JUNE 21

Do your best and let the chips fall where they may. Stressing will not shift the chips.

-From the Queen

A message from the queens

JUNE 22

On the cloudy days,
stay focus on the sun
hiding behind the clouds.
Before long the sun will
come out again.

-From the Queen

A message from the queens

JUNE 23

I embrace my unique, journey that I am on and I have the strength to overcome any challenges that comes my way with God involved leading me every step of the way breaking chains and doors opening with over flowing blessings, with Good health and right mind.

-Mildretta Peterson
A.K.A
Doll Light

JUNE 24

The moment you accept you for you, BEAUTY would have just blossomed!

-From the Queen

A message from the queens

JUNE 25

No matter what the storm looks like, just keep walking. God is the umbrella that shields you.

     -*Doll Mesmerize*

A message from the queens

JUNE 26

Stop wasting time trying to find yourself and spend time creating YOU!

-From the Queen

JUNE 27

It's okay to disagree and to be disagreed with.

-From the Queen

JUNE 28

You don't NEED make up to make you beautiful. Your heart does that all by itself.

-From the Queen

A message from the queens

JUNE 29

LIFE

When life is touched by a shining light, only beauty can come from it. When life is touched by darkness, the world feels the effects left behind. The positive people that are brought into your world, is a direct result of the light that you cascade unto others. Be that bright light for someone.

-ROLENCIA GARRISON-CUFF

A message from the queens

JUNE 30

Don't live your life based on the opinions of others.

-From the Queen

JULY

Colossians 1:10

"We ask this so that you will live the kind of lives that prove you belong to the Lord. Then you will want to please him in every way as you grow in producing every kind of good work by this knowledge about God".

JULY 1

I have good energy, and anyone connected to me will receive my good energy as well.

-From the Queen

JULY 2

Do not create a fantasy of lies to comfort you when the reality of the truth is looking you in the face.

-From the Queen

A message from the queens

JULY 3

Hello, my sister or brother is reading this. I am BabyC Lake.
I love you; Jesus tells us to love our neighbor in the bible. *Leviticus 19:18*
We are all beautifully made by our maker.
We are gifted and have our own callings. Find it and live in it.
Remember that you are more powerful than you know.
Walk in peace knowing that Christ spirit lives in you.
One of the things we lack from this earth distractions is loving one another.
Compliment your brother or sister instead of hating.
Let's spread love.
Have you ever heard never judge a book its cover?
It's true that something or someone can look one way but the inside or the reality could be a whole different story.
Only God knows your story from beginning to end.
I encourage you to continue walking by faith and not by site.
Only God can judge and that is the only yes, we need. He chose us so that we would have eternal life.
So why not choose him.

Choosing God,

-BabyC

A message from the queens

JULY 4

If God told you to do it, you don't need anyone's permission to execute it.

-From the Queen

JULY 5

I will pay my debt. I will be debt free. I will owe man nothing. I will make wise business decisions. I will not live above my means. I will think about how I spend my money. I will seek financial wisdom.

-From the Queen

JULY 6

You are a big deal.
Remember that.

-From the Queen

A message from the queens

JULY 7

I am deserving of Love, Good Health and Success!

—Tyrell Vinson

JULY 8

The one thing you should understand for a better life is WHO YOU ARE.

-FROM THE QUEEN

A message from the queens

JULY 9

The attack is not against you,
it's against your
ASSIGNMENT!

This sentiment echoes the spiritual reality talked about in Ephesians 6:12

Ephesians 6:12
"For we wrestle not against flesh and blood, but against principalities, against powers, against the rulers of the darkness of this world, against spiritual wickedness in high places."

The enemy knows that the assignment that God has placed on your life is so POWERFUL that he will stop at nothing to get you to call it quits. The bigger and greater the assignment the harder the enemy will come at you.

You must stay focused and stay the course. Don't allow anyone or anything to get in your way. The enemy can't stop you; he has no power to do so. The only person that can stop you is YOU. If you quit, you will lose.

To fight the attack, you must put the whole armor of God on so that you will be equipped for anything the enemy comes at you with. Don't allow him to move or shake you from fulfilling the assignment given by God. (Ephesians 6:10-18).

Jesus never gave up and don't you do it either.

From
Dawn Hannon

Facebook:
Visual.Motivation

JULY 10

It's okay to take selfies of YOU
It's okay to get dolled up for YOU
It's okay to work out for YOU
It's okay to go shopping for YOU
It's okay to buy YOU something just because
It's okay to take YOU out on the town
It's okay to take YOU on vacation
It's okay to take a moment for YOU to nap
It's okay to take care of YOU
IT'S OKAY TO...YOU

-From the Queen

A message from the queens

JULY 11

Life experiences are stepping stones to your future, learn from them and create your own wonderful opportunities.

-Crystal Jackson-Crowder
A.K.A
Doll Allure

A message from the queens

JULY 12

Gracious words are a honeycomb, sweet to the soul and healing to the bones.

De'ja Boyd

JULY 13

More time spent with God helps you make wiser decisions.

-From the Queen

A message from the queens

JULY 14

You are enough and have everything you need right now, just as you are.

-Metich Hagans
A.K.A
Doll Extraordinaire

A message from the queens

JULY 15

If you don't want to do it than don't do it. Just remember it's YOU that have to deal with the consequences, good or bad.

-Jahleah Benjamin

A message from the queens

JULY 16

Trust God's timing. God's timing is always perfect. God is redirecting you for something new and greater.

-Monica Benjamin

A message from the queens

JULY 17

Embracing your uniqueness and practicing self-love are such powerful habits. You are indeed worthy of love, respect, and all the beauty that shines from within and outward.

Tell yourself: I am gorgeous!
Keep celebrating yourself!

Teresa Turner
A.K.A
Doll Treasure

JULY 18

I AM
Bold because God says I am
I AM
Beautiful because God says I am
I AM
Bountiful because God says I am
I AM
Brave because God says I am

-From the Queen

A message from the queens

JULY 19

Your spirit is rare, and you were chosen with a purpose. Your light brightens every room, and you are never in darkness, for you were made to shine.

Tanzi Minnis
A.K.A
Doll Virtue

A message from the queens

JULY 20

I'm Still Standing Because I'm Not Easily Broken

and

YOU ARE TOO!

With love from

Nicole Hargraves

IG: Nicole Hargraves

A message from the queens

JULY 21

BE AT THE READY

I encourage you to trust in the Lord always and include him in everything you do. Your breakthrough requires obedience. "Be At The Ready" for the move and blessings of God over your life.

God is a promise keeper. Do not miss your appointment with destiny!

       Be At The Ready!

Blessings,
Ms. Melinda Nogieru, MBA

Owner and Founder,　　　　Owner and Founder,
The Heart of A Lioness　　　Be At The Ready LLC

www.theheartofalioness.org　　www.beattheready.com

JULY 22

You are an amazing woman, and everything you're doing is leading you toward your dreams. Remember that every step, no matter how small, is progress. You've overcome so much already, and you're stronger than you realize. Keep believing in yourself—you have the power to achieve anything you set your mind to. Don't give up, you're so much closer than you think.

-Angie Driskell

A message from the queens

JULY 23

I am resilient and equipped to face any challenges that come my way. With each adversity, I grow stronger and more adept at navigating difficulties.

ETHEL QOH BUCKHAULTER

A message from the queens

JULY 24

I affirm that I am aligned with my highest purpose and my grateful heart is a magnet that attracts everything I desire. I lack nothing. Abundance, love, wealth, health, peace, success, finances, resources, and positive energy flows through me and to me, easily, frequently, and freely.

~ *Phoenix Ascar*

JULY 25

Hey listen…
You already got
what it takes!
You just have to
believe it!

-From the Queen

JULY 26

Understand this and don't ever forget it…
You can be the *kind* person that you are, with the good heart that you have,
AND STILL SAY…
NO.

-From the Queen

JULY 27

Don't be a person that is trying to impress.
Be the person that is focused on progress.
But don't apologize if your progress is impressive.

-From the Queen

A message from the queens

JULY 28

Look in the mirror and repeat:

I am
Confident,
Courageous
Cute
Charismatic
Controlled
Conscious
Creative
Changed

-From the Queen

A message from the queens

JULY 29

I am in control of my:
ATTITUDE
and my
EFFORT

-From the Queen

A message from the queens

JULY 30

I am everything God called me to be!

"Don't sit down and wait for opportunities to come, get up and make them!"
-Madam C.J. Walker

Tanya Terrell

A message from the queens

JULY 31

You have the strength to rise again. Each day is a new opportunity for healing and growth. Remember, it's okay to take your time; your journey is uniquely yours, and brighter days are ahead.
Speak aloud:
I am capable, confident, and full of potential. Every challenge I face helps me grow, and I trust myself to succeed indeed.

From the heart of
Princess Cato

AUGUST

Matthew 22:37

You shall love the Lord, your God, with all your heart, with all your soul, and with all your mind. This is the greatest and the first commandment.

A message from the queens

AUGUST 1

I am stronger than any storm; I choose to create, not destroy. My purpose is creation. God's grace loves, protects, and blesses me. I am blessed, empowered, and filled with new might. Now is my time, my turn. I am a champion, and I am she.

Angela Harris-Tucker A.K.A Queen B

A message from the queens

AUGUST 2

Everyone gets tired but there's a difference between resting and quitting.

-From the Queen

A message from the queens

AUGUST 3

Yes, you've been through some challenging obstacles, but you made it through. You are working hard for a better life. You are doing your best to stay strong, ambitious, and resilient. No matter where the road leads you, know that you are valuable, and you deserve to succeed. So do just that!

-From the Queen

A message from the queens

AUGUST 4

Focusing on changing your world will help change the whole world.

-From the Queen

A message from the queens

AUGUST 5

You are a resilient and determined individual who works hard, perseveres through challenges, hold your head high with confidence, and seek guidance from the Lord. Giving up is not an option for you, and you will not be defeated! The blessings from the Lord continue to surround you, and with faith and perseverance, you will overcome any obstacles that come your way. Keep moving forward with strength and positivity.

-Wanakee McKenzie Miller

A message from the queens

AUGUST 6

Note to self:
Although I may fall
I will continue to walk,
run and crawl, to meet
my goals and achieve
them all.

-From the Queen

A message from the queens

AUGUST 7

I am pretty smart
I am pretty strong
I am pretty forgiving
I am pretty cool
I am pretty prefect for me!
Yes, I'm just pretty!

-From the Queen

A message from the queens

AUGUST 8

You are NOT the negative opinions of others.

-From the Queen

A message from the queens

AUGUST 9

You are the one.
It is in you.
So, walk in it.
Show it.
And be unapologetic for it!

-From the Queen

A message from the queens

AUGUST 10

Let your heart be full of love, goodness, forgiveness, compassion, wisdom and caution.

-From the Queen

A message from the queens

AUGUST 11

My energy is one of the prettiest things about me.

-From the Queen

A message from the queens

AUGUST 12

Don't worry about anything; instead pray about everything. Tell God what you need and thank Him for all he's done.

-Kieshia Ruffin

AUGUST 13

Today look in the mirror and say:

No matter what the day looks like, I got this and no one or anything will stop me from accomplishing my dream!

-From the Queen

A message from the queens

AUGUST 14

I didn't deserve half of the crap I have endured, but it is obvious that I was built to make it through it all because I'm still here.

-From the Queen

A message from the queens

AUGUST 15

Take a moment to tell yourself:
I am beautiful and I am strong, and I can do anything I set my mind to do.

-From the Queen

A message from the queens

AUGUST 16

I alone unbrace the truth of who I am. I have welcomed the wisdom that has given me growth.

-Marcia Hicks

A message from the queens

AUGUST 17

Romans 8:18
For I reckon that the sufferings of this present time are not worthy to be compared with the glory which shall be revealed in.

-Jasmine Brown

A message from the queens

AUGUST 18

Never let someone else tell YOU who YOU are!
SHOW them who YOU ARE…
A Woman's ROAR!

-*Debra Francois*

A message from the queens

AUGUST 19

Once you accept who you are, the game will change.

-From the Queen

A message from the queens

AUGUST 20

It okay to live in peace. It's a peaceful place.

-From the Queen

A message from the queens

AUGUST 21

Repeat this three times today:

I can.
I will.

-From the Queen

A message from the queens

AUGUST 22

Never be apologetic for deciding not to be sad and choosing to be powerful, creative, full of love and an illuminating light.

-From the Queen

A message from the queens

AUGUST 23

My mother's favorite song was.
" I Almost Let Go"
These lyrics bring me strength to this day!
"I almost let go. I felt like I couldn't take life anymore. My sickness had me bound, depression weighed me down, but God held me close so I wouldn't let go, God's mercy kept me so I wouldn't let go. I almost gave up. I was right on the edge of a breakthrough, but I couldn't see it. The devil thought he had me, but Jesus came and grabbed me. He held me close, so I wouldn't let go. So, I'm here today because God kept me. I'm alive today only because of his grace. God kept me. He kept me. "
These words kept me going during my darkest days. You see I survived a deadly, aggressive, hard to treat cancer. There are days when I didn't want any more chemo. I told the doctor please stop all treatment I will accept what happens to me. But God said fight on I got you! So whatever fight you are in, never give up God's got you!

-Sheryl McCoy

A message from the queens

AUGUST 24

Just don't stop!
Just don't stop!
Just don't stop!
Just don't stop!
JUST DON'T STOP!
JUST. DON'T. STOP!

-DJ Just Do it

A message from the queens

AUGUST 25

Yes, life is tough
But let me enlighten you
on something…
So are you!

-From the Queen

A message from the queens

AUGUST 26

It is said that death and life is in the power of the tongue.
Which do you use your tongue for?

-From the Queen

AUGUST 27

Be the woman that is quick to fix another queen's crown rather than being quick to tell others that it is crooked.

-From the Queen

A message from the queens

AUGUST 28

I am enough for me, and I am worthy of whatever I desire, more importantly, I am grateful for each and every day, I thank God every minute.

-Amy Jacobs

A message from the queens

AUGUST 29

Confidence is not about always being right.
It is about not being afraid to be incorrect.

-From the Queen

A message from the queens

AUGUST 30

GIVE THANKS!

Give thanks in everything. When I wake up in the morning and place my feet on the floor, I give thanks. I give thanks to God with my whole heart and a grateful heart. When I think about God and how good God is, I can't help but give him thanks!

Psalms 136:26
O give thanks to the Lord of heaven for his mercy endureth forever.

GIVE THANKS!

-Karen Stith-LaBoo

A message from the queens

AUGUST 31

Love is Priceless:
True Love is Extraordinary.
If you are lucky enough to
find that one true love, hold
on to it with your life.
If you find it twice YOU are
truly BLESSED.

-DonEsther Morris A.K.A Doll Conquer

SEPTEMBER

Romans 8:28

And we know that in all things God works for the good of those who love him, who have been called according to his purpose.

A message from the queens

SEPTEMBER 1

You can't lose a battle that you've already won!

Let God be the muscle operating your tongue!

Love,
Donna MH Robinson
A.K.A
Big Sis Speaks!

www.mybigsisspeaks.store

A message from the queens

SEPTEMBER 2

Change favors the prepared mind, so it is incumbent upon us to be as cognizant of our path as we can and be open to the blessings in our future! With that comes a sense of purpose and joy that knows no bounds!

www.latonyareeves.com *-LaTonya Reeves*

SEPTEMBER 3

I AM NO LONGER:
Broken
Fearful
Sad
Empty
Worried
Powerless

I AM:
Bold
Fierce
Strong
Enough
Worthy
Powerful

-Lisa "Doll Glam" Noell

I AM WHO I AM
I AM A CHILD OF GOD AND
THAT MAKES ME AMAZING!

A message from the queens

SEPTEMBER 4

I AM ME BECAUSE OF THEE! I'M NOT HER,
I AM SHE!
LET ME BE, IF YOU'RE NO GOOD FOR ME!
YES I AM SHE,
THE WOMAN GOD MADE ME!

ON TODAY, TAKE SOME TIME FOR SELF AND LEARN WHO SHE IS, TAKE A WALK IN THE PARK, TREAT YOURSELF TO A NICE DINNER AND ALWAYS REMEMBER YOUR WORTH!

PSALMS 139:14
I AM FEARFULLY AND WONDERFULLY MADE!

-Chinnetta Richardson

A message from the queens

SEPTEMBER 5

Inspiration is the spark that ignites creativity and drives us to achieve our goals. It can come from anywhere, at any time, and often when we least expect it.

Inspiration has the power to transform our lives and lead us down new and exciting paths. It is a vital force that pushes us to be our best selves. Motivating us to make a positive impact on the world.

On this day, find inspiration in everything that you do!
Seek it while reading a new book, listening to music and *especially* while checking yourself out in the mirror!

You are worth it!

-Trena Ross

SEPTEMBER 6

Stop focusing on your past. It is just what it is, your past. Looking back at what was, keeps you from focusing on what is *now* and what is to come.

-From the Queen

A message from the queens

SEPTEMBER 7

God can bring you back from anything, so do yourself a favor…
RUN YOUR LIFE, RUN YOUR BUSINESS AND LET GOD BLESS.
AND DON'T FORGET TO PRAY DAY AND NIGHT!
Loving you always
Michelle 'MeMe' Lovett

IG: MEMEALLOVER2
WWW.MICHELLELOVETT.COM

A message from the queens

SEPTEMBER 8

Happy, peaceful people tend to be the prettiest and most beautiful people.

-From the Queen

A message from the queens

SEPTEMBER 9

I am filled with Self - Love

I am filled with clarity.
I am filled with inspiration.
I am filled with awareness.
My life is filled with opportunities.
I am filled with abundance.
My life is filled with strength.
My life is filled with blessings.

-Reine Jenique

A message from the queens

SEPTEMBER 10

My affirmation: is for women on their journey to healing and finding themselves again...
I have some rules that I set in place for myself during this process as I'm still healing and walking, talking and living this journey with you every day.

1. Opening my eyes every day is a blessing and thanking GOD is how I start my day every day.
2. Asking for help is a sign of self-respect and self-awareness.
3. Changing my mind is a strength, not a weakness.
4. I alone hold the truth of who I am.
5. I'm allowed to ask for what I want and need.
6. I am Good and Getting better everyday
7. I am Loved and Worthy of it.
8. I AM OPEN TO HEALING BECAUSE TODAY IS A NEW DAY.
9. My healing journey is not complete.
10. I must do the work, because God love me, and I love me too.

To all my beautiful sisters stay blessed on your healing journey and remember I love you.

-*Terri Stevens*

A message from the queens

SEPTEMBER 11

My worth is not in anyone
or anything.
The value of my worth lays
within myself.

-From the Queen

A message from the queens

SEPTEMBER 12

I will not get weary and give up, but I will keep on running the path that God has for me. John 10:12 tells how a hired Shepard leaves when things get too chaotic, but we are to stand firm on the promises. I will not flee when things get hard, but I will endure because I know that God will see me through it all, according to His will.
1 Corinthians 15:58 Therefore, my dear brothers and sisters, stand firm. Let nothing move you. Always give yourselves fully to the work of the Lord because you know that your labor in the Lord is not in vain.
Do not give up, what you do matters.

-Loretta Brooks

A message from the queens

SEPTEMBER 13

MY LOUISIANA GRANDMOTHER ALWAYS SAID, "C'EST EN SIROP!" – LIFE IS SWEET.

YET, MY JOURNEY TO MOTHERHOOD PROVED OTHERWISE. AMIDST THE HIGHS AND LOWS, I FOUND STRENGTH IN PRAYER AND SCRIPTURE. IT'S A REMINDER THAT EVEN WHEN LIFE ISN'T SWEET, THE CREATOR IS THE SOURCE OF ALL GOOD THINGS.

-TARMARIA DAVIS

FACEBOOK: TARMARIA DAVIS

A message from the queens

SEPTEMBER 14

The standards you set for yourself is how people will respect you.

-From the Queen

A message from the queens

SEPTEMBER 15

You say...
I am a powerhouse ready to seize the
moment and shine boldly.

-Arvilla Beckworth

www.arvillabeckworth.com
Social media: @arvillabeckworth

SEPTEMBER 16

The pain you overcame is because of the power that is within you.

-From the Queen

A message from the queens

SEPTEMBER 17

Life is: 90/10

90% of what may have happened to you can be contributed to life life-ing. But how you respond it is the 10% that is most important.

-From the Queen

SEPTEMBER 18

The moment you fuel your confidence with belief in yourself, you will begin to GLOW.

-From the Queen

A message from the queens

SEPTEMBER 19

Rule number one to maintaining your peace:

F------- WHAT THEY THINK!
(YOU FILL IN THE BLANK)

-From the Queen

SEPTEMBER 20

Small progress each day will add up to big success one day.

-From the Queen

A message from the queens

SEPTEMBER 21

"What you are is GODS GIFT to you!
What you become is your gift to God"
Make every effort to add to your faith goodness; and to goodness, knowledge (2 Peter 1:5)
-Nikki Taylor

Instagram:the_queentaylor
Facebook: Nikki Taylor

A message from the queens

SEPTEMBER 22

LIFE. GRACE.

And let us not grow weary of doing good, for in due season we will
reap, if we do not give up." *Galatians 6:9*

You are the gardener of your life, take time this season to allocate space for personal growth. Prioritize self-care, water you and nurture your well-being. Today, contemplate, on the path that led you here and do so without judgments. Refrain from self-criticism, focus on your progress and trust the process. You possess everything necessary for this moment, express gratitude and appreciation regardless of the circumstance. In this instant, harmony exists, so whatever life plants you bloom with grace because the choices you make will determine your growth and flourishing.

-*NEAT CHANEY*

www.Iamneatchaney.com

SEPTEMBER 23

It is absolutely okay to allow space to feel and process my emotions. I will operate at my optimal level in every area of my life. I am not a victim. I am victorious!

-Mona Jackson

A message from the queens

SEPTEMBER 24

I am Beauty at its best. With my best effort, I can never fail. I move forward, becoming the best version of me.

-Doll Creole

A message from the queens

SEPTEMBER 25

Happiness is a mood
and
Peace is a mindset.
Embrace both.

-From the Queen

A message from the queens

SEPTEMBER 26

The moment you feel like giving up, look at everything you have overcome. And that is the moment you realize that you can't give up!

-From the Queen

SEPTEMBER 27

Wishing for it is good.

Believing for it is great.

BUT

WORKING for it makes it happen.

-From the Queen

A message from the queens

SEPTEMBER 28

The term
"Built Ford Tough "

As it pertains to endurance and progression was appropriate moreover Ford was built after us!
(*BLACK*) WOMAN TOUGH!

In life when you are getting tackled keep pumping your legs never stop pushing through!

-TRULY TRACY
'MINNIE'S DAUGHTERS'

SEPTEMBER 29

Be proud of yourself. You are doing it. It doesn't matter the speed at which you are doing it. Stop looking at what you don't have. Stop complaining about how hard it is. Simply be proud of yourself because no matter the storm, the pain, the fear, the doubt, the unknown, you are getting it done. So take a moment and simply be proud of YOU!

-From the Queen

A message from the queens

SEPTEMBER 30

One of the most beautiful things in the world that you can do is
BE YOURSELF.

-From the Queen

OCTOBER

John 16:33

I have said these things to you, that in me you may have peace. In the world you will have tribulation. But take heart; I have overcome the world.

A message from the queens

OCTOBER 1

Embrace Your Power, Own Your Journey

In a world that tries to define us, remember that your true power lies within. You are more than the roles you play or the titles you hold. You are a force of nature, capable of greatness, not just in spite of challenges, but because of them. Every experience has shaped you into the resilient woman you are today. When you look in the mirror, see the strength, wisdom, and courage within. These qualities define you—not others' opinions or limitations.

Empower Yourself: Your voice matters. Speak up, stand tall, and never let anyone dim your light. Embrace your true self, and the world will recognize your brilliance.

Encourage Each Other: We thrive when we lift each other up. Celebrate successes, support in need, and build a community where every woman feels seen, heard, and valued. Together, we are stronger.

Inspire Action: Don't wait for permission to live your life. Take bold steps, even when they scare you. Trust in your ability to navigate challenges, and know each step brings you closer to the life you deserve.

Motivate Yourself: When the road gets tough, remember why you started. Keep your eyes on the prize and let your passion drive you forward. You have the power to turn dreams into reality—one choice, one action, one day at a time.

Push Towards Greatness: Greatness is a journey. It's in the small, consistent actions that build momentum, the courage to keep going when others quit, and the belief that you are worthy of your dreams.

To every woman reading this: *You are powerful, capable, and worthy.* Let's rise together, not just to meet challenges but to exceed them. Greatness is not just a possibility, but an inevitability.

With love and solidarity.
Arica Quinn

OCTOBER 2

Anyone can get dressed up and become eye candy but only a person of wisdom can be soul food.

-From the Queen

OCTOBER 3

There is no better representation of BEAUTY than accepting you for you.

-From the Queen

A message from the queens

OCTOBER 4

Life is precious, make sure you spend time with people who DO NOT want to live this life WITHOUT you!
-*Ronnisha Ross*

Facebook:
Ronnisha Ross

A message from the queens

OCTOBER 5

Be UNSTOPPABLE: Your goals are waiting for you; you simply must go after them!

-Makara A. Jones
VSU Essence of Troy
Cosmetologist/Lash Tech

A message from the queens

OCTOBER 6

In the shadows, where hope seems thin and frail,
The road is long, and the night is deep,
But if you keep moving, if you refuse to fail,
Through the struggle, a brighter dawn you'll reap.

-Osunjii Yeldell

Facebook: Osunjii Yeldell

A message from the queens

OCTOBER 7

Three positive attributes a woman should have intact:
Her mind
Her attitude
Her class
　　　Repeat:
Believing in myself makes me unstoppable.

−From the Queen

A message from the queens

OCTOBER 8

IN THIS LIFE YOU WILL BE SUBJECTED TO SITUATIONS THAT YOU DIDN'T KNOW THAT YOU WERE IN. BUT THE ONE THING YOU HAVE TO ASK YOURSELF IS. WHAT WAS THE LESSON? IT'S A PART OF THE JOURNEY THAT GOD HAS GIVEN YOU TO MOVE YOU.
SO, MAKE SURE YOU PAY ATTENTION.

-Vanessa Henderson

A message from the queens

OCTOBER 9

Self-respect

I am proof enough of who I am and what I deserve, I deserve self-respect and a clean space.

-Cherylita D. Cobb
A.K.A
Doll Opulence

A message from the queens

OCTOBER 10

It is humbling to know that I can be replaced but it is even more humbling to know that there is no one like me.

-From the Queen

OCTOBER 11

I am strong I am wealthy I am brave I am beautiful in Gods image and with help from God I will have success in all I was created to do.

- *Alana Alves*

A message from the queens

OCTOBER 12

I AM WHO GOD SAYS I AM.

I AM A WINNER WITH THE HEART OF A LIONESS.

I am not left behind; I am on time and have exceeded the boundaries and restrictions that people put on me. What I carry is not containable. It will overflow everywhere I go, and no one will be able to dim my light for God is with me always.

-Ms. Melinda, MBA

A message from the queens

OCTOBER 13

No matter how it is looking, I know that everything is working out for my good.

-From the Queen

A message from the queens

OCTOBER 14

I know that my struggle has challenged my strength.
I see that I am stronger than I thought I was.

-From the Queen

OCTOBER 15

So what! It didn't work, it didn't turn out how you wanted it to. Dry your tears, stop complaining! Get up and try again. It doesn't matter what happened. You can do it!

-From the Queen

A message from the queens

OCTOBER 16

-Genet Thomas
IG @official_na3

"I will praise thee; for I am fearfully and wonderfully made marvelous are thy works; and that my soul knoweth right well."

Psalm 139 :14

A message from the queens

OCTOBER 17

If anyone does not compliment my life in a way that makes it better, they have to go.

-From the Queen

A message from the queens

OCTOBER 18

She's committed to grow her nurturing soul. She's patient and fully understand her inner qualities which are: Strength Empowering Multitasking Self-awareness. She reflects and grow. She's loyalty, committed and overcomes obstacles. She is dedicated, supportive beautiful and radiant. Her lights glows. She has self-love self-acceptance and grace. She walks with elegance, dignity. She is energetic, passionate and her wisdom, experience insight and intuition are like a powerful, feminine, energetic Divine Goddess. She's like a beautiful flower, one of kind. She is love. Her love is unconditional. She celebrates her worth. She vibes, and flows like a river. Her light is bright. She is transforming grounded, nurturing, and life-giving. She embraces stress with the word of God. she is humble through the storm recognizing her beauty and diversity while celebrating her victory. She is unique. She is different.
She is the essence of a woman.

-Sparkle

A message from the queens

OCTOBER 19

Loving me is not selfish, it is necessary.

-From the Queen

A message from the queens

OCTOBER 20

I CAN DO ALL THINGS
THROUGH Christ THAT
STRENGTHED ME.
- Philippians 4:13

-LaJoyce Lewis
Facebook: LaJoyce Lewis

A message from the queens

OCTOBER 21

Thank you, mom, for giving birth to a:

Brave
Beautiful
Smart
Kind
Special
Loved
Resilient
Capable
Wonderful
Intelligent
Successful
Caring
WOMAN

-From the Queen

A message from the queens

OCTOBER 22

I do this for
ME,
MYSELF
and I first,
and that's okay.

-From the Queen

OCTOBER 23

Loving me first doesn't mean I am selfish. It just means that I understand the importance of making sure I am loved.

-From the Queen

A message from the queens

OCTOBER 24

Life is beautiful! Stand firm and never give up because you are WORTHY!

-*Carmen Lynum Wright*

OCTOBER 25

I am strong, I am enough, I am a warrior who will always conquer life's battles, and I am freeing myself from all destructive doubt and insecurities.

Arianna Alves

A message from the queens

OCTOBER 26

After all the na-sayers, after all of the doubters, after all the tears, after all of the whining, self-doubt, the constant roadblocks, I remind myself that I must

DO ~~N~~T

~~QU~~ IT

-From the Queen

A message from the queens

OCTOBER 27

She is clothed with strength and dignity; she can laugh at the days to come.

-Proverbs 31:25

A message from the queens

OCTOBER 28

When you can accept that you are not important to some people that is the moment you are bondage free.

-From the Queen

A message from the queens

OCTOBER 29

You are worthy and you deserve nothing but the Best! Never give up on yourself! Continue to strive to better than you were yesterday. You may fall, but remember, some failures happen to make you stronger!!

PHILIPPIANS: 4:13: You can do ALL things through Christ which strengthens you!

-Phyliss Spearman

A message from the queens

OCTOBER 30

Peace sent you a message:

Silence is better than unnecessary drama.

Protect me.

Love,
Your peace.

-From the Queen

A message from the queens

OCTOBER 31

Everyone does not deserve you so stop giving yourself away. Knowing your value will eliminate unnecessary hurt.

-From the Queen

NOVEMBER

John 13:34

"I give you a new commandment, that you love one another. Just as I have loved you, you also should love one another."

A message from the queens

NOVEMBER 1

I Pray...

I pray that little girl who keeps everything to herself heals.
The girl who thinks nothing she does is significant enough to share.
Who would care?
Who would show up for her?
I pray that fatherless little girl knows it was never her fault,
And stops blaming herself.
Having a man will never define her worth.
She is enough!
I pray that little girl who cannot stay out the Pantry finds a better way to deal with disappointment, rejection and neglect.
I pray that little girl on her back realizes that too much too soon can kill all her unborn dreams.
yearning for love and attention in the wrong position is dangerous.
I pray she forgives herself.
I pray that depressed little girl learns time will not standstill for her, she has to open up and let her blessings in.
I pray the little girl that's now all grown up knows the world is waiting for her.
And it's time to give the people what they want!

-Tammy Michelle

A message from the queens

NOVEMBER 2

The realist thing I can admit to myself is that I know for a fact that God is the ONLY reason I made it this far.

-From the Queen

A message from the queens

NOVEMBER 3

I have made up in my mind that I will be as happy as I want to be.

-From the Queen

A message from the queens

NOVEMBER 4

Sometimes you may feel like a sad caterpillar but always remember you are a beautiful butterfly!

Maliyah Clore aka LeLe

A message from the queens

NOVEMBER 5

I give myself permission to thrive not just survive.

Courtney Clore aka CeCe

A message from the queens

NOVEMBER 6

Never ever stop being the best version of yourself that you can be.

-From the Queen

A message from the queens

NOVEMBER 7

It's your dream,
It's your vision,
It's your faith.
Do not wait for
anyone else to make
it happen.

-From the Queen

NOVEMBER 8

There is no comparison between the moon and the sun. They each have their own purpose. They each shine when it's their time.
The moral of the story: Stop comparing your life and or your success to someone else's. Your success is for you and theirs is for them.

-From the Queen

A message from the queens

NOVEMBER 9

Whatever you do in life, do it as unto the Lord *(Colossians 3:23-24)*. Sometimes you may feel overwhelmed with the requirements, expectations, and vicissitudes of life.
When challenges weigh you down and you feel like you can't go on.
BREATHE.
Remember your purpose and reflect on the positive impact you're having on others.

-Glenda Y. Carswell

A message from the queens

NOVEMBER 10

Don't give advice you wouldn't use yourself.

-From the Queen

A message from the queens

NOVEMBER 11

If you don't like the path that you are on. Change your path.

-From the Queen

A message from the queens

NOVEMBER 12

Stop being afraid of the very thing that will set you free or help you to succeed.

-From the Queen

NOVEMBER 13

Don't let negative people ruin your mood.
Doing so gives them control over your mental state.

-From the Queen

A message from the queens

NOVEMBER 14

Every day, I'm a better version of ME.

-From the Queen

A message from the queens

NOVEMBER 15

I see me as a butterfly.
I am easy and beautiful to look at but not so easy to catch.
I know my value.

-From the Queen

A message from the queens

NOVEMBER 16

Never be afraid to lose, because if you do, you'll never try, and then you will always lose. Trust God with your life.

With love from
Tenacity Love

Facebook: Tenacity Love
IG: tenacitylove
Facebook:N'Satiables Catering

A message from the queens

NOVEMBER 17

You are Beautifully and Wonderfully made in the Image of God.

<u>SPEAK</u>   your Truth with Love and Authority.
<u>STAND</u>   tall in all of your Glory. Let your Beauty
<u>SHINE</u>   from the Inside… Out.
<u>WALK</u>   Proudly in your Purpose, and
<u>LIVE</u>   your life with the Dignity of the Queen that you are.

-DonEsther Morris A.K.A Doll Conquer

Dedicated to my Daughter's, Granddaughter's, Cousins (female) and Nieces

A message from the queens

NOVEMBER 18

"Best Self"

God first. In this life journey, we each, have a unique path, destined by opportunities to learn, grow and become the best version of ourselves. Self-improvement is beyond being about achieving external goals or meeting societal expectations; it's about understanding and harnessing your key potential. Imagine the person you aspire to be; that vision is a reflection of untapped desires and capabilities. Courage and commitment is needed to take the necessary steps for fulfillment. By doing so, not only contours "your" future but also improves the lives around you.
You Matter.

-Georgette Coleman-Ford

Facebook .. Georgette Ford (Jetta)
Instagram.. modestmomapparel
YouTube.. @GeorgetteTV1
TikTok.. @georgettetv1

A message from the queens

NOVEMBER 19

As I keep my hands in his hands I know I have a friend when life seems the darkest I have a friend when I'm unsure of the path that I'm taking I have a friend when the path that I'm taking is rocky and unsafe I know I have a friend when there's no one to encourage me to go on ,that you can do it I have a friend that tell me I can do all things through Christ who strengthen me I have a friend who will never leave me or forsake me yes I have a friend, I look to The hills from which cometh my help, my help and strength comes from the Lord, my friend.

-*Karen Stith-LaBoo*

A message from the queens

NOVEMBER 20

My dreams are bigger than me that is why I rely on God to help me make them become a reality.

-From the Queen

A message from the queens

NOVEMBER 21

Don't throw back the stones people throw at you, collect them and build your empire.

-From the Queen

NOVEMBER 22

It's OKAY
If today is not a good day
If today you made a mistake
If today you are not your best self

It is also OKAY
To take a moment for you to regroup
To take a moment to make decisions that is best for you
To take a moment to do you

-From the Queen

A message from the queens

NOVEMBER 23

Today I promise to protect my peace, mental, emotional, and spiritual state of mind by avoiding people with negative, unhealthy energy.

-From the Queen

A message from the queens

NOVEMBER 24

I am BEAUTIFUL
I am STRONG
I am WORTHY,
and
I am more than enough.
I rise above challenges
and
I embrace my power
with courage and
confidence!

Doll Faith

A message from the queens

NOVEMBER 25

Your transformation may be painful, but you will not fall apart instead you are just falling into something different with a new capacity to be beautiful. For me it was my hair, I learned that I am not my hair.
Yes, Alopecia may have stolen my hair, but it didn't steal my beauty, and neither will the trails of life steal yours.

-Belinda Gordon
A.K.A
Mahogany

A message from the queens

NOVEMBER 26

I refuse to allow society to dictate my value as a person.

-From the Queen

A message from the queens

NOVEMBER 27

I Am above and not beneath
I Am the head and not the tail
I Am more than a conqueror
I Am the lender and not the borrower

No Weapons formed against me shall prosper
And any tongues that rise up against me shall be condemned

I Am loved by God
I Am chosen by God
I Am protected by God

Kendra Nicole
Website:
www.vipsocio.com/market/classy-k

NOVEMBER 28

I love myself too much to ever allow myself to be misused, abused, or mistreated.

-*Nina Ramsingh* A.K.A Doll Fearless

A message from the queens

NOVEMBER 29

I see *me* girl.
Through all the crap and life's obstacles and even some of my poor decisions, I am still standing, I am still holding on, I am still moving forward, and I will succeed.
Because for me failure is not an option.

-From the Queen

NOVEMBER 30

Note to self:

I will spend time with people that is good for my mental health.

-*From the Queen*

A message from the queens

DECEMBER

Romans 12:10
Love each other with genuine affection and take delight in honoring each other.

A message from the queens

DECEMBER 1

This year, I choose a path of happiness and wellness.

In Agape Love
-*Sharon R. Bowie*
A.K.A
Doll Brite Eyezz

A message from the queens

DECEMBER 2

I know God is always here with me that is why I can smile through the storm.

-From the Queen

DECEMBER 3

The best revenge:
1. Kill folks with success,
2. Bury them with a smile and
3. Annihilate them with your peace.

-From the Queen

A message from the queens

DECEMBER 4

Never be anyone's option. It demeans your value.

-From the Queen

A message from the queens

DECEMBER 5

I AM worshipper I AM NOT A worrier.

-From the Queen

A message from the queens

DECEMBER 6

Motivate yourself, do not wait on anyone to motivate you because at the end of the day only you can do it!

-*Justice Carswell*

A message from the queens

DECEMBER 7

GURRRLLL,
Ain't nobody going to do this but you. Pull on your inner strength and get it done. People are counting on you!

-Thadnechia Stith

A message from the queens

DECEMBER 8

Your journey of "Best Self" certainly won't be a straight path but will hold both challenges and successes. Our greatest strengths are often discovered in overcoming obstacles. Embrace these moments; as they serve as stepping stones to your growth. Not sure where to start; well, think about some achievable goals that align with your values and passions. These should inspire you and push you out of your comfort zone. Progress might start off slow; and setbacks are inevitable; however, no matter how small, every effort you make is a testament to your dedication of desiring a better self. Celebrate your milestones and use them as a motivational tool for forward movement. Your journey to becoming your "Best Self" is a gift to you and the people around you. Be the authentic you and Know Your "Best Self" then be the "Best Self" You Know.
You Matter.

-Georgette Coleman-Ford

A message from the queens

DECEMBER 9

I always say, 'the lesson is in the look back'. Always find the reason why...in all that you do AND all that has happened to you. When times get hard, faith, family and prayer will strengthen you. Never lose hope.

Psalm 27
"The Lord is my light and my salvation..."

-*Stephanie Ruffin*

DECEMBER 10

There is more than one way to get to the store.

The moral of the statement is:

Sometimes change is necessary.

If the plan is not working, change the plan, but don't change the goal.

-From the Queen

A message from the queens

DECEMBER 11

I am a STRONG and POWERFUL (black) woman, who has risen above many of life's challenges.
Devil step aside for I am a child of God!

-Annette Heathington A.K.A Doll Integrity

A message from the queens

DECEMBER 12

I AM THE DRIVING FORCE IN MY LIFE!
PURPOSE IS MY FUEL!
MOTIVATION IS MY BATTERY!
CONSISTENCY IS MY ALTERNATOR!
I AM DRIVEN!
I WILL STAY ON COURSE!
I WILL ACHIEVE MY JOURNEY!
Repeat 25 times each day for 30 days!

-Felicia "Transition" Winston

IG: mirproductions804
FB: mirproductionsrichmond

A message from the queens

DECEMBER 13

I am 10 years old, and I really love acting. The first time I started acting, I was really nervous. I did not know what to say. I had so many lines.

It all started with me doing my own one girl show. I developed four characters all on my own! One was '70s girl. another I played myself; one was very classy; another one was a nerd.

How they all the characters started off, was me just going into my Gigi's closet. I put on some fancy clothes of hers. I went up to her and I said," Hey Gigi look at me." My Gigi got so inspired that she called a cool director named Sista Jay Jay. I performed my one girl show. Everyone loved it! Even one of my friends came from my school.

My dad had passed away earlier that year, so I dedicated a song to him in the show. People started crying. Some parts they were cheering. That's when I realized I could affect people's emotions with my acting. So, I studied and practiced acting. I got better and better. So never give up on your dreams no matter how nervous you are at the beginning. Your gift can help others! So don't be afraid to share your gifts!

-Sherle Walker

A message from the queens

DECEMBER 14

Always remember that there is a Rainbow at the end of the storm. And please stay connect ed to the Vine that connects to the Root (GOD) the Lord of the world. No matter how things seem to look like always find something positive in everything. Amen.

-Annette Parker
A.K.A
Doll Integrity

A message from the queens

DECEMBER 15

REAL IS RARE, SOW RIGHT! TO REAP the RARE REALITY of what YOU made REAL!

— By Nwaebo

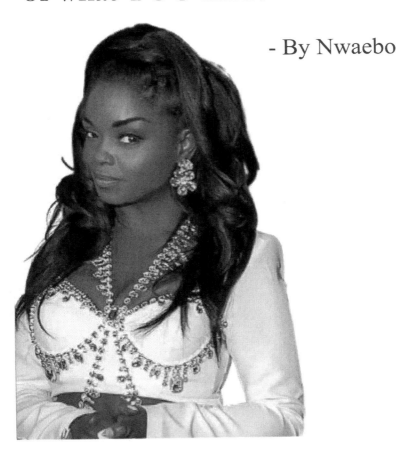

A message from the queens

DECEMBER 16

Just take a moment and think...

Can you see with your mind's eye people living together with plenty of water and food, no more hurricanes or bad weather, no more sorrow or pain, no more crying and no one dying. All sharing in the blessings God has ordained each of us, living life without an end and all we lost will be regained and our hurt and misfortune will be forever lost in the past, remembering the last battle God brought you through as a testimony and a message to your enemy that he is better you nor can he touch you. Bottom line; don't let your ship sail by you without you on it.

Monetia Smothers

Dedicated to Morris
and Blanche Smothers

IG: msexqfullfigurega2018
www.armanientertainmentgroup.online

A message from the queens

DECEMBER 17

My mind is too delicate to allow negativity to enter into it.

-From the Queen

A message from the queens

DECEMBER 18

Confident is the ability to admire someone else's beauty without questioning your own.

-From the Queen

A message from the queens

DECEMBER 19

Faith is not just about hoping for it. It's about what you are doing to receive it.

-From the Queen

A message from the queens

DECEMBER 20

"Lord, you don't have to move this mountain, just give me the strength to climb. Lord, don't take away my stumbling block, just lead me all around it."
-Psalms 40:8

"I delight to do thy will"

Love,
Maxine S. McDaniel, Director

Facebook:
Tickled Past Pink Foundation, Inc.

Facebook:
Maxine Simmons McDaniel

DECEMBER 21

Focusing on what you can't do hinders you from seeing what you can do.
Psalms 46:5 says God is within her. She will not fail.

-From the Queen

A message from the queens

DECEMBER 22

His joy will give you the strength you need to make it through. So, rejoice, dear one. Rejoice!

-Kwana King-Stark

A message from the queens

DECEMBER 23

Stop trying to fit in. You were created to stand out! Embrace you!

-From the Queen

A message from the queens

DECEMBER 24

In a world moving faster than the speed limit, she chooses to move at a pace that will help her win her own race.

She is one with the Creator who breathed life into her, standing on a foundation of peace, purpose, and unwavering faith.

She trusts in the timing of her journey, that was predetermined while being formed in her mother's womb, knowing that every step she takes is divinely guided.

She is not rushed by the world around her; instead,

she remains grounded in the present moment, aligned with her true path.

Her pace is her power, and in her stillness, she finds strength. SHE IS *YOU*!

-Jane Johnson

A message from the queens

DECEMBER 25

Lord, place me where You can use me and align my heart with Your purpose. Heal my mind, body, and spirit. Thank You for growth, maturity, and wisdom. Help me stand firm and secure in who I am. Transform me for a lifetime so I may pour out Your gift of love onto those I encounter daily.

-Teke Addison

Facebook- Teke Addison
IG: @Carlissa.t and
@DreamWalkerDesigns

A message from the queens

DECEMBER 26

I accept that if it's God's will, it will happen, and nothing can stop it. However, if it's not God's will, I know God has something better for me. And I accept that.

-From the Queen

A message from the queens

DECEMBER 27

Sometimes life is like an ocean —
find someone to ride the waves with you.

Love you always momma
-Genda

A message from the queens

DECEMBER 28

I DON'T...

Just hear, I listen
Just talk, I act
Just tell, I show
Just correct, I encourage
Just take, I give
Just read, I comprehend
Just feel, I love

-From the Queen

A message from the queens

DECEMBER 29

I will not give anyone the power to take my peace, my confidence, my will, my dignity or my strength.

-From the Queen

A message from the queens

DECEMBER 30

Words of encouragement for the grieving and brokenhearted:

To every parent who has endured the unimaginable pain of losing a child, know that your grief reflects the depth of your love and the joy they brought to your life. Though they are no longer with you physically, their love and light remain in your heart. Continue to love, heal, and honor their memory as you keep moving forward. The bond you share will never fade.

Alva Jenkins-Houston

Facebook: Alva M. Jenkins Houston

A message from the queens

DECEMBER 31

Repeat after me…

I am now becoming all that I want to become!

Love,
Joyce White
IG: Jaylee48

A message from the queens

I pray that the affirmations, letters of encouragement, scriptures, testimonies and words of love have helped you throughout the year.
May something, we have written helped to better your life, make it through trying times and motivated you to live your best life.
Remember YOU come FIRST! So, love yourself FIRST, receive God's love FIRST and live the life that makes you happy FIRST.
And in case no one has told you lately, you are loved!

-Sista Jay Jay

FOLLOW SISTA JAY JAY ON ALL SOCIAL MEDIA AT
I AM SISTA JAY JAY

A message from the queens

For more great reading visit www.raggirlpublishing.com

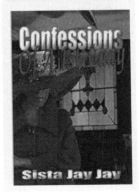

A message from the queens

A message from the queens

R.A.G GIRL PUBLISHING THANKS EACH COLLABORATING AUTHOR. YOUR WORDS WILL LIVE FOREVER!

Made in the USA
Columbia, SC
24 November 2024

47050584R00213